To the Tellison Family,
True friends past
and future!
Merry Christmas!
much love,
AP 94

LOOKING FOR #1

Portraits and Passions
of Nashville Songwriters

Photography by Dee Davis
and Biographies by Annie Price

Copyright ©1994 by Dee Davis and Annie Price.
All Rights Reserved.

Eggman Publishing, Inc., 2909 Poston Avenue, Suite 203, Nashville, TN 37203

Printed in the United States of America
First trade printing: November 1994

Book design by Maryglenn McCombs and Mike Walker

Cover design by Mike Walker and Hatch Show Print

All film processed by Chromatics in Nashville, Tennessee

Hair stylist: Kim Johnson

Makeup Stylist: Elizabeth Lee

Library of Congress Catalog Card Number
94-61840

ISBN 1-886371-05-9

Preface

If you buy an album and don't read the liner notes, you're missing out on the heart of the music. Read the names in parentheses under the song title. Those are the song's writers. That's where music starts.

To get a "cut" in Nashville is a glorious thing. It means an artist believed in a song enough to record it. If you're a songwriter and you get a cut, you get some respect. If that song is released as a single, you get attention. If the song goes to #1, you get a lot more of both. Plus a lot of money. Those are the benefits, but not the reasons writers write.

They feel. They think. They listen. They dream.

But if you took away the music, could you still hear the passion? That's the purpose of this book: to capture the reasons, the inspirations, the sacrifices, all without a note. Just film and ink.

Any night in Nashville you can walk into the famous Bluebird Cafe, Douglas Corner, or any other club in town and see people like this. Some of them have written monster hits. Some have never gotten a cut. But they're all looking for the same thing: a voice for their passion, a cut, a hit, and even a #1.

DEDICATION

The prose in this book
is lovingly dedicated to the memory
of my Grandfathers:
James William Price,
who gave me the genes for writing, and
LaSalle Fowler,
who gave me the guts.

DEDICATION

All of the photographs in
this book are dedicated to my Dad,
Maclin P. Davis,
who has always dedicated so much to me,
and without whom none of this,
nor much else, would be possible.

Andy Arrow

"A" is for "Andy," "A" is for "Arrow," this book's Alphabetical, and that's why he's here. It is a difficult task to describe what a songwriter is. Perhaps it is easier to say what a songwriter is not. Andy is not. He'd rather play guitar. But if it weren't for songwriters, Andy wouldn't have a job. No songs, no gigs. He'd just sit around looking glum. Like this. So, like Andy, we all owe our employment or enjoyment to the people on the following pages. Please continue.

Larry Beck

Larry is a loser. "I'm good at losing stuff," he says. He lost his mother and his aunt. Then his girlfriend left. A hurricane took his house. That was back in Charleston, his hometown. But look at this guy since he brought his guitar to Nashville. Things are still a little backwards, but better. Loss is inspirational. Songs need inspiration. Larry needed a girlfriend. He got one. But he says she's not as good as the last one.

Laura Chandler

This was the advice she got about coming to Nashville: "They said dress conservatively, so I got a haircut." A well-known singer/songwriter in San Francisco, Laura is slowly making inroads to Music City. The day we took her picture was her first day in town. Laura does not play country, but said she received a warm welcome. "Nashville gives songwriters respect on every level," she says. From her visitor's perspective, she found the songwriter's community to be warm and encouraging, but just competitive enough to be healthy. "Nashville prizes its songwriters. There's no place like it in the country."

Beth Nielsen Chapman

When she wakes up in the morning, she is not confused. There is a clarity that has been left by the slow settling of a muddy grief. Her husband died. That he could go, and she could go on has given her monumental perspective, an intense understanding of life. Red is redder, blue is bluer, funny is funnier, truth is truer. "I am extremely in touch with the journey," she says. Every song she's written, every hit she's had, has come from a patient and honest heart. Now unencumbered by "ought to's" and "should have's" that heart is steering Beth towards delightful ideas. Clarity. How pleasing and how precious.

Jameson Clark

There is a girl in South Carolina who is crying over this boy. Sure, she's got his pledge of matrimony, but when he shows off the pictures in his wallet, he brags most on someone else: Alan Jackson. Like his hero, Jameson is chasin' that neon rainbow. And it's nice to have a photo of Alan to glance at when there's more rain than bow. Jameson writes songs that are "straight, down home country" Traditional is his taste. For young Mr. Clark dreams of being a member of something Grand and Ole: The Opry. He does not, however, carry any pictures of Little Jimmy Dickens.

Ellen Crandell

You have to use a little imagination here. It's a metaphorical pose. Songwriting is so personal that you have to be willing to bare it all. Metaphorically. Allegorically, actually. Ellen writes story songs, the kind that come from personal experience but translate well to other people's lives. And she's good at it. Suzy Bogguss put one of her songs on the *Aces* album. Though she was a little self-conscious, Ellen was gracious enough to be our living literary device. Literally, we thank you, Ellen. You make a mighty marvelous metaphor.

Tim DeBolt

"I am the desert ghost." Wandering this earth alone, he is a man without peace or a place. Agressive, abrasive, a bit melodramatic, Tim says he has trouble fitting in. Maybe it's because he's learning how to play the bagpipes. Loneliness, muscle, and sex are his muses; songs his trustiest confidants. For Tim, there is little other relief. "Nothing is calming."

Dean Dillon

Laugh if you can, cry if you must. Rarely has such jubilation been born of such misery. Abandoned by his father and shuffled around his family as a child, Dean didn't know where he belonged. . .until he found music. "I belonged to that pen and that paper and that guitar." He hitchhiked to Nashville. A fiery writer, a notorious drinker, he won and lost three record deals. But he always poured passion like whiskey into his music. And the cup ran over. He's written ten #1 hits for George Strait. Revived and redeemed, today Dean is one of Nashville's most revered writers.

Judd Erickson

Some people will sacrifice everything to give Nashville a shot. Judd walked out on his fiancé. For seventeen years, he fronted bands in Minneapolis playing his own original songs. But it wasn't getting him where he wanted to be. Nashville could. "I didn't want to grow old kicking myself for not trying." With a glimmer of interest from one record label, he made the move in early '93. Judd says he mostly writes sad songs about relationships. Leaving his has been woefully inspirational. "I got a lot of songs out of that, but no regrets."

Mona Faith

Mona's mother gave her guitar lessons when she was a little girl, but she didn't want to learn. Thinking a toy ukulele might be less intimidating, Mom tempted her with four strings instead of six. Mona left it in the sun and it melted. Then she met a man who made her strings ring. Now Mrs. Faith is a hot ticket at hot luncheons and banquets in her home town of Hampton, Virginia. She's written over 200 country and gospel songs and lists an alphabet of affiliations: GMA, BMI, NSAI. Now she's Mama's pride, and Don Ho's disappointment.

K.K. Falkner
Pat Gallagher

DON'T TRUCKLE! (truk'l) v. to be servile; submit. K.K.'s hobby is reading the dictionary. Pat's hobby is searching for spelling and grammatical errors in public advertisements. A semantically correct pair, they are. They met scraping boat bottoms in Newport Beach, California, and decided there must be life beyond barnacles. Now they're "Pat Gallagher and the Atomic Playboys." K.K. is the "centerfold singer." When it comes to music, they don't truckle, buckle, or knuckle under. Allies of alliteration, rivals of perfect rhyme, it's commando composition: "Say what you gotta say, make it honest, make it rhyme, make it rock, and get it over with."

Steven Farmer

Steven has come a long way from two different directions. From knee deep in dung as a manure shoveler on a Montana feed lot, to the safe yet sanitary confines of medical studies in college, Steven didn't like the future either path promised. So, when the road forked, he took *neither* of the roads less taken. Instead: I-40 East to Nashville. Since 1984, he's had one firm course: shovel the imaginary manure, stay in the proverbial songwriter school, and get some major cuts. He's got three boys to put through college.

Harvey M. Freeze

Harvey wears a hat, and he always has. He's not claiming to be a real cowboy, but he's like one. He's been broke like a cowboy. He lost his wife like a cowboy. And he lost his truck like a cowboy. He says he can't ride, but he can fall. He's got a brother named Harlan who sings rock music and was even on *Star Search*. But this boy breathes the bayou. New Orleans Country, cherie. Shipyards and beer, Louisiana l'amour. That's "The Harvey Thing."

Arlene Gold

It don't mean a thing if it ain't got that western swing. Sho'nuf, this little lady from the Big Apple wants to put a little saddle swagger in her big band swing. But not to sing; it's a writing thing. Arlene makes a living fronting big bands, but she really wants to be a country COMPOSER: to write a song of enduring quality. In short, in tall, for the history of it all, Arlene wants to be the Gerschwin of country music.

Cliff Goldmacher, John Tirro, Jen Cohen

This is a picture of the music industry: the way it begins and its tender, earthy roots: Collaboration. Cliff, John, and Jen are each pursuing independent goals with different visions and voices. Cliff writes folk-rock; John anything from rag to jazz; and Jen sings the hell out of every song she finds. But no one makes it alone. The night this picture was taken, John and Jen backed up Cliff for his set. The night this picture was hung at the Bluebird, John and Cliff played for Jen. That's how it works in Nashville. Each seed in the row shares the sun and the rain. And when they do flower, they have each other to thank.

Adie Grey

The dulcimer is a delicate instrument. It is simple, yet classic. Its parameters for musical experimentation are narrow. But Adie likes the cozy confines of its limits. It's easy to play. That way she can concentrate on the lyrics. Refine the details that make a song extraordinary. Usually, Adie writes a song quickly, as if the idea, melody, and words come in a giftwrapped package. It's the unwrapping that takes time. "Songs need reworking *always.*"

Liz Hengber

"What! You want I should dress up or some-
thin'? Look, I'm just me. A displaced Brooklyn
housewife. Okay, so I don't got a husband but
I will soon. I'm learning to cook. I can shake
and bake chicken like an earthquake in L.A.
It's the Cheerios side dish that's a little dicey.
But, y'know, hey. As long as Reba keeps cutting my songs, I'll be fine. If not, I'll put on
something pink and join the Ice Capades.
What?! Did you call me tacky? Tacky? Thank
you."

John Mark Higginbotham

This songwriting thing is just like a relationship. John Mark and success are flirting with each other, but they just can't seem to commit. They're trying to get together, but he needs to find himself first. And there's so much temptation, he just wants to play the field. He's got a date with the blues, a call in to folk, and a little crush on Polka. How can he go steady with just one style? He just wants his songs to be loved. Is that so wrong?

Jerry Holland

Jerry is from the toughest city in America: New York. He's broken his nose, his ribs, every finger, every toe, and another guy's jaw . . . teaching karate. PEACE is Jerry's ultimate goal. Right now he is exploring a path to harmony through music. But he says that's not the only way to find it: "This is a selfish pursuit. I try to justify it. I know my calling is ultimately something else. I am karmically compelled to be here now." Jerry is prepared for songwriting success or failure: "I'll try something else."

Marcus Hummon

"Only love sails straight from the harbor, and only love will lead us to the other shore." He wrote those tender words for Wynonna. He wrote them because of his family. It's not hard to write songs with inspiration like this. Love is a way of life for Marcus, his wife Becca, and their three year old son, Levi. Marcus is proof that good words and good will pay off. He's landed an artist deal with Columbia Records. That life is hard, full of long and bumpy roads. But he can't leave his inspiration behind. There will be bunks on the bus for his wife and son.

Amanda Hunt-Taylor

She's just *got* to know the weather. Whether to stay inside, or get out and walk. So the weather channel is usually on, whether her husband likes it or not. Now, her husband Rick loves her whether the weather forecast is ugly or fine and she loves him whether the weather rains or shines. That love inspired her to write "Your Love Amazes Me," but she doesn't remember whether the weather was nice or not on that day. However. Love knows no weather, though it sees many whethers. They endeavor! Whether the weather, they'll weather the whethers, 'cause they're tethered together forever and ever.

Andie Jennings

This is not a hobby, it's the mindless accomplishment of a songwriter's frustration. For six years, Andie's been doing something productive, though not necessarily socially redeeming, with her writer's block: That is a 200 foot long chain of gum wrappers. "It's like a diary," she says. During happy times she used Carefree fruit-flavored wrappers. During the bad, Clark's. The chain represents gum-ption and neuroses, two fine qualities in any songwriter. Andie says it will take a good man or a lobotomy to make her break the chain. But she hopes it happens before she reaches the world record, which is 7,000 feet. "I'm not that neurotic."

"Jellyroll" Johnson

That's a lot of heavy breathing on the floor. A pile of harmonicas that this gentle-looking man has blasted out, blown away. If your song needs soul, you call Jellyroll. He's got wail and moan made to order. He's tried songwriting, but the harmonica is a melody instrument. It's too limited for chords. Plus, your mouth's preoccupied so you can't sing. That's why he stuck to what he does best. Playing. Now he's one of the sharpest harpists in town.

Miranda Louise Johnson

Ten hours a week Miranda waits tables at the famous Brown's Diner. 120 days a year she sings in clubs around town. The remaining 200 odd days are unaccounted for. Best guess is she's probably cryin', wailin', worryin', or wishin'. Miranda has the blues. She's got them real good. Complete with rhythm and soul. She's opened shows for Gatemouth Brown, Albert Collins, and Albert King. She's recorded an independent album, but the girl still ain't happy. She wants a deal. And some shoes, and more blues.

J.K. Jones

She met Smokey Robinson because he had a backache. J.K. is a massage therapist, but really a poet. She studied classical piano, forgot it all. But thanks to her guitar and her now publisher Smokey, she's a hit songwriter. She and Billy Dean co-wrote his single, "I Wanna Take Care Of You." She moved to Nashville from Malibu in 1993, and it's revived her happy, playful spirit. She's been relying on her imagination to write sad songs. But she has to if she wants to see her dream come true: "I wanna hear Vince Gill sing something I wrote."

Jamie Klee

The guitar is pink, the hat is white, and the attitude is red. She voted for the young Elvis stamp, because she likes his "big hunk o' love" raw energy. She's got a Chris LeDoux cut, but her main focus is producing. Her studio is decorated in a funky '50's style, and she likes to record the way they did back then: live. No. Jamie's not an artist, but, yes, she always wears boots. And a hat, too. Because it looks so damn good on her, that's why.

Sandy Knox

Success is so beautiful. Especially when its perks come full circle. Sandy used to work as a makeup artist; and a bartender, and a chef, and a waitress. But there is only one thing she ever really *was*: A songwriter. She knew it and so did her parents. At her lowest times, her folks always believed. "If you give up now," said her mom, "you have a 100% chance of failing." Since 1992, she's written three smash hits for Reba McEntire. She's holding pictures of her parents to say "thank you." The rest says, "Yeah, when you hit the top, there's a little bit of glamour, and a hell of a lot of fun."

Ron LaSalle

Ron is a writer who believes the writing's done. Melody, meter, and lyric exist, just wandering and wondering who will write them down. But songs only come when there's room for them to fit in our lives, so you gotta clear some space. How? Face death. Nothing clears your mind like skydiving, or swimming above Niagra Falls. What is thrilling and chilling is ultimately inspirational. If you want to meet the muse, you gotta make the invitation. "We're all just antennas; our job is to stay alert."

Bill Lloyd

Bill was a pretty good student in school. He had a B+ average if you didn't count math and science. Those courses had too many rules. See, Bill is better at ambiguity. A right-brain thinker, he prefers to extract fact from the abstract. To be exact, he seeks that emotional "moment of clarity." It's the place where words and feelings somehow sort into a rhyme. After cuts by Suzy Bogguss, three albums from his collaboration with Radney Foster, and now his own solo release, Bill knows this: There aren't any rules for making good songs. Let's keep it that way, shall we?

Deborah Lonrau

"Trichnosis, psychosis, cirrhosis of the liver. Tuberculosis, halitosis, my last boyfriend had 'em all." That's the kind of lyric you'd expect from the woman who wrote "I Want To Kill My Neighbors Upstairs," and "Stereotypical Episcopal." Ask Deborah about songwriting: "Don't bore 'em." Ask her about cooking: "Don't choke 'em." Indeed her byline is frequently found in the "Food" section of *The Tennessean.* So whether tune or tuna, serenade or marinade, ballad or a salad, Deborah certainly slings the savory and the silly.

Layng Martine, Jr.

Elvis, Reba, Kathy Mattea. They know the guy is a hitmaker. But even if you're successful, you still gotta stretch. Reach for the stars, or at least the ketchup. Layng loves restaurants. Diners are divine, grills are simply thrilling for soaking up culture and conversation. Sometimes he takes his napkin home scribbled with ideas and song titles. It may take a while for them to simmer in his subconscious, but when the song is cooked, it comes out good and hot.

P.S. That's not his dog, but pugs are always lookin' for scraps.

Tom Mason

"Um-ba-da-da, Um-ba-da-da, Tuff luck a lotta. Um-ba-da-da, Um-ba-da-da, Wish me luck a lotta." Tom's writing has matured since this first composition at age three. But the sentiment remains. Especially since he says he can't find any decent Thai food in Nashville. But what he has found is Truth. Beauty. Color. Canvas and stone. As an Art Preparator at the Cheekwood Museum of Art, his eyes are cast on parallel crafts. He hangs paintings, moves sculptures; and finds words in their forms. If you listen to his songs, he hopes you'll see art, too.

Duane Michaels

Accordion to Duane, the accordion is very difficult to play. But since the age of five, he has stretched and squeezed notes: Cajun, jazz, and classical stylings. An internationally important instrument, the accordion has taught him to sing in Italian, Czech, German, and Spanish. Tucked near his heart, he wears a reminder of his Catholic faith: A medal of St. Jude Thaddeus, the Patron Saint of Hopeless Cases. Duane says four out of five prayers to the Saint have been answered: a solid marriage, a squelched wild side, good health, and a good dog. There's just one prayer left: a record deal.

Brian Nash

He just threw it all away. He was a big shot New York advertising executive with an MBA from Dartmouth pulling down good dough for selling tuna, cat food, and fancy clothes. "I had a moral crisis with advertising," he says, so he decided to follow his bliss. Bliss to Brian is bleak and depressing songs with imperfect rhymes and unhappy endings. Ah, doesn't that feel better? Yes!

Pam O'Daniel

She's Rebel's daughter. She didn't know him well, but she's heard stories about him from the hobos who did. Rebel rolled on tracks over ties across plains and hard times. A Santa Fe Railroad boxcar was Pam's home. It is no wonder that years later and miles away, she writes songs about trains, broken love, and homelessness. She has a social agenda ratified by experience. Pam can't remember Rebel. But she won't forget him either.

Jeff Pearson

When he's not doing it, he's thinking about it. Or reading about it. Jeff says it is thrilling, the essence of excitement. He's so hooked, he does it four or five times a week: Bass fishing. The strike, the fight, the capture. And ultimately, always, the release. There is tremendous respect in this endeavor. Those fish are friends, playmates. That's how it is with the musical muse. An experienced and published songwriter, Jeff believes inspiration doesn't just swim up to you. You have to befriend it and fish. And when it strikes, put words to paper. For the fish will surely cut *you* loose.

"Phillybilly"

It's a big door to bust down, that one to the country music castle. But if you work together, you've got a better chance. Joe Collins, Richard Fagan, and Kacey Jones have each had major artist cuts: George Strait, John Michael Montgomery, and Mickey Gilley. But as "Phillybilly," they're writing for keeps...for themselves. "This just clicks," they say of their collaboration. "It's something undefinable." Phillybilly is a lesson in the mystery of music. And an example of how patience and persistence pays off.

Gene Pistilli

You don't recognize him? How about by his alias: Hank Sinatra, Jr.? No? He's really quite famous. Gene was the goalie for the Staten Island Stingers dart team, a famed mafioso figure who rode shotgun on a "hot dog wagon," and a highly decorated American Astronaut. Okay, so he's prone to a little hyperbole. Gene was actually a founding member of the Manhattan Transfer, and the author of the 1989 ASCAP Song Of The Year "Too Gone For Too Long" recorded by Randy Travis. His hobbies include smoking, swearing, and sulking. His main inspirations are alimony, child support and trying to impress Jodie Foster. Sure, you may know a lot about him now, but he says "Nobody *really* knows me 'til they taste my sauce."

Dave Pomeroy

Bass-ically, you get the idea. Or maybe not. You see, the bass is a poorly understood instrument. It's not just the noise that rattles your windows, it's the sound that vibrates straight to your core. Each bass has a place, and Dave has taste. He knows when and where to use each one. He can make them sing or sigh, punch or growl. One of the most demanded session players in Nashville, Dave is also an accomplished songwriter...of instrumentals. He's planning to release an album of songs that show off the versatility of his instruments. The tentative title: *The Day The Bass Players Took Over The World.*

Alan Rhody

Plug it in and get it out. Wouldn't it be great if you could just hook that amp straight into your heart? Let the emotion roar without fiddling with chords and lyrics. Alas, music needs a medium, and Alan's in the middle. His subconscious stewing; his heart churning, brewing. Alan is a Nashville hitmaker. Lorrie Morgan, Ricky Van Shelton, George Jones, Tanya Tucker, and The Oak Ridge Boys. They've all cut his songs that cut to the heart. The best songs are personal, he says, and the hardest to get out. He may not have a phono jack in his chest, but he's got something better: talent and discipline.

Bo Riddle

Bo has too much talent. He is blessed and bummed. He wishes his trade were his hobby, and his hobby his trade. Without qualification, Bo is one of the best custom boot makers in the world. He makes his living outfooting Nashville's stars. But you outta hear Riddle fiddle. A lightning-fingered and lively entertainer, he'd rather be known as a world class musician. He writes songs, too. But it's hard to chase your first love when your second is so good to you. And it's hard to love your second when you're cheating on your first. He's cursed.

Perry Rohrer

At any given time, this man had access to over one million pens and 36,000 reams of paper. He's seen oceans of white out, and twisting printer ribbon rivers. As the manager of an office supplies warehouse, Perry couldn't escape the feeling that he should be writing. So he packed up his family and told Lancaster, Pennsylvania, to find its own stick-um notes. His ink-stincts were right. In just two years he's had several single song contracts, and is close to a full-time publishing deal. Make a note of that.

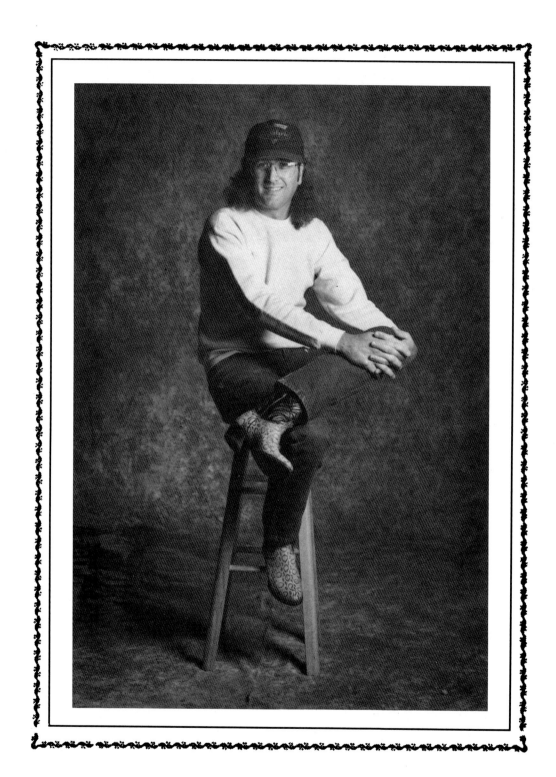

Kyle Rullmann

Before you grill bratwurst, you should boil it in beer. And don't write about a teenage crush on your second cousin. "That song sucked." These are the truths that Kyle discovered. This Wisconsin Cheesehead homogenized with Dixie in 1987. He sold vacuums and pizza, and now is a lighting grip for music videos and movies. But he also runs the soundboard at the Bluebird Cafe. He's listened and learned, and says he's writing better. And now he knows another truth: How can you tell if your song is good? If someone asks to hear it again.

Sam Russell

If you think the fashions of the '70's were an embarrassment to the cultural history of America, you can blame Sam. He used to run a hippie clothing store in San Francisco. Luckily, he loved rock and roll more than platform soles. Raised in Lake Tahoe, Sam spent years playing the casinos and resorts. He made good money, and he always played originals. In 1992 he moved to Music City to become a better writer. He says it's working, especially since he hears so much good music tending bar at the Bluebird Cafe. He's so excited about writing that he's even started a book: *Didactic Murmurings of a Butthead.*

Daniel Ryan

The melodies come quickly, but the lyrics take longer. The weight of the words is a heavy responsibility. Daniel is a compassionate man with an earnest belief that music helps mend a sore heart. And a sore world. He is already a healer, a successful Chiropractor. But he left his California practice to write songs in Nashville. He says he's just trading one healing work for another. "I want to make this world a better place," he says. So Daniel has abandoned his comfort, forsaken all certainty. Tender his intent, steely his resolve.

Jan Schim

If wishes were horses, beggars would ride. If horses were wishers, they'd beg you to write with the heart and conviction of their beloved Ms. Schim. The steeds are pleased to have Jan as a groom at the Brass Lantern Horse Farm. She loves each creature and the ground they walk on. "I've always been an environmentalist," she says. Neither animals nor earth can speak for themselves. So Jan's plan is to stand as a beacon for both. Two causes, six strings, one voice.

Victoria Shaw

From the ballad queen who brought you "I Love The Way You Love Me," "Too Busy Being In Love," and "The River," now comes a frantic dose of frenzy. Rhyming crisis? Pronoun problem? Adjective adversity? Get on the phone! Get out of the house! Just do lunch! Don't force the issue, wait 'til it hits you. Call up a pal and get your mind off the grind. She'd do the same for you. 'Cause friends don't let friends write junk.

Jim Sherraden

Sometimes dreams come true, but not exactly the way you'd planned them. Jim knows that first hand. A wildly successful printmaker, he manages Nashville's famous Hatch Show Print. With wood block letters and hand-turned presses, Jim keeps the art of classic show posters alive. But that career was his second choice. He wanted to be a songwriter in Nashville. Nashville didn't want him. But Europe did. Thanks to an association with Norwegian pop star Jonas Fjeld, Jim has over forty cuts abroad and won two Scandinavian Grammies. It didn't take long to wash away his disappointment with Nashville. The ink comes off easy, too.

Tia Sillers

It will not rain, it would not dare. Not on her. Tia is a woman of considerable talent, control, and accomplishment. She holds degrees in English and Fine Arts. She didn't start writing songs until she was in graduate school where she earned an MBA. She was a Professor at the University of North Carolina, and also taught persuasive speaking at Belmont College. She was offered a gig in international banking but turned it down to pursue music at home in Nashville. "My parents cried," she said. But in nine months she had a publishing deal. She's 26.

Marshall Stern

Weary and no seat. It's not the first time he's had to improvise. Marshall is a professional clown. Nose and paint and shoes and wig; the facade of "Frenchy." Marshall says, "He's an idiot." But he pays the rent. Pluck off the nose. Wipe away the greasy color. Go further inside. He can't hide, but he tried. He didn't want to write; it's too hard. But he's good at it. Ricky Van Shelton cut one of his songs, but dropped it from the album. So Marshall keeps writing. It might pay the rent. "I'm an idiot, too."

Sylvia

Smoky the dog was named after "Smoky the mountains." Sylvia says he brings out the child and the mother in her. She takes a nurturing approach to her writing, both for the song and the listener. Her writing is expressive and unguarded, but not patronizing: a little allusion here, a little innuendo there. Listeners are smart enough to figure out a song's meaning, and how it applies to their lives. An RCA recording artist in the mid 80's, Sylvia's looking for another deal. Though it's frustrating, you are what you are, you do what you do. She's a musician. There really aren't any other options.

Wes Taylor

Real good barbeque requires a shower after-wards. Wes knows 'cause he's a connoisseur. And an inventor, too. He's forged two board games and a personal toothpick dispenser called "Pickpocket." With all that wisdom and creativity, this real live ranch hand from the Rockies is looking for a deal. Wes wants to be an artist, but he still writes. Mostly about women. Here's what he says makes a song good:

1) Energy.
2) The music makes the words mean more.
3) Garth Brooks wants to help you finish it and make it his next single.

Verlon Thompson/Suzi Ragsdale

They say to write about what you know, so they do: Love. Verlon and Suzi have been writing and living partners for four years. Trisha Yearwood, Joe Diffie, Billy Dean, Suzy Bogguss: they've all cut a Verlon or Suzi song, or a Verlon *and* Suzi song. The duo has written some great duets. Especially for themselves. They're currently touring to promote their own independent CD release. Their ultimate goal? Says Suzi: "Happiness." Says her husband: "To keep Suzi happy."

Erik Thorson

Every time Erik gets up to play at Douglas Corner he starts his set by saying, "Rhonda says Hi!" The crowd responds, "Hi, Rhonda." It's been the routine for years. But some regulars have become skeptical: Is there really a Rhonda? Yes, there is. And a little Lars, too. They are the people who give Erik the courage to continue in a business that seems to tease him relentlessly. He's had several artists cut his songs, but never had a hit. So he substitute teaches and tries out new songs every Tuesday at Douglas Corner. He always tells Rhonda that the folks there say "Hi."

Alice Townsend

Alice collects people. Having friends is a much more satisfying hobby than having lots of things. That's the kind of philosophy she got growing up in rural South Carolina. That's the kind of song she writes: three minute novels about friends in small towns. She's expecting a new friend soon: a little girl. The mother of two boys already, Alice is feeling a new wind of spunk and vigor as her daughter's arrival draws nearer. "I'm gonna show her what girls do," which is anything and everything. Including writing great songs.

Jon Vezner

Words have weight. Even the simplest shouldn't be tossed about lightly. Nimbly arranged, a simple phrase can weigh heavy on the heart. He's proven that with "Where've You Been," "Time Passes By," and "A Few Good Things Remain," all recorded by his wife Kathy Mattea. Jon is a deliberate man, an intentional writer; each word thoughtfully chosen. But it's not easy. "Writing is like therapy. Or like scratching an open wound." It's the greatest release, the most intimate secret revealed.

Katie Wallace

Katie has a recording contract on Honest Records, because that's the way she is. Honest. And strong, and determined, and outspoken, and good. She's had songs cut by Neal McCoy and Billy Ray Cyrus. But now it's her turn. She's not afraid of Music Row, but it may be wary of her. "The establishment has a problem with women who display strength," she says. Katie does. "I can't help it." She says there's a real need for women who are real, and she's stepping up to the challenge. Listen for her first single. It's called "Hard Woman to Love."

Jim Williams

Cuts, cuts, cuts. Hits, hits, hits. This man knows what he wants. From Village Of Custards, Pennsylvania, Jim left on a jet plane...U.S. Air, to be specific. That company thought he'd make a fine employee. Jim thought "cuts, hits, cuts, hits." He founded "Silly Notions Promotions," his own publishing company. And he brought his cool guitar. It's an old Sears Craftsman made of Brazillian rosewood. It's worth about $5,000. But he'd trade it for hits and cuts.

Without Adam

Fame is a rosy fruit, fortune its rummy taste. Them apples have caused a lot of trouble, historically, but these women aren't afraid to chew through the serpentine music biz. Playing their alternative rock originals, Ree, Chris, Joli, and Renee draw hip crowds at Nashville clubs. "People love to see four chicks just wearin' it out," they say. About their name: "We're not sacrilegious at all." Their first moniker read Genesis more generously: "Eve Was Framed."

Paul Zografi

He has studied the greatest minds of all time. Pondered the theories of thinkers and thoughts. Paul has a degree in Philosophy. His favorite thesis comes from the philosopher Schoepenhauer: "Life is flowing. Ever changing, full of renewal and rebirth." Paul says that's how his music is. Simple, spiritual, evolving. There's one other thing you need to know about Paul: He's a cook at the Bluebird. Try his Cajun catfish. "It just tastes good."

The Universal Writer

This is your homework assignment. Everything you need to write a great song is in this picture. Just put yourself in it. Take courage from the pages before. Every composer started with this big empty space. Whether hits or misses, published or un-, there's one thing that all true songwriters have in common: *They try.*

Dee Davis would like to thank. . .

Annie Price, for liking this crazy idea
Mark Tucker, for inspiring me to set my goals entirely too high and my deadlines entirely too short.
Mark Irwin, for introducing me to so many of these songwriters whom I've come to admire.
Jennifer Bennett and Kim Fischer who each showed up just in time.
Scottie Hill Belfi, for showing me the sources from which I drew the energy to do this book.

Annie Price would like to thank. . .

Dee, my "Pug Partner," for asking me to write.
The staff of TNN Country News for cutting me miles of slack and tolerating my panic.
Jay Barron: A whiz in the biz.
Ruth Scott Belfi: The "one good idea" found me.
And Marilyn Nordlund for being a tough high school English teacher. You're making a difference.

Special Thanks To. . .

Our benevolent and protective publishers, Eggman Publishing, especially Richard Courtney and Maryglenn McCombs.
Amy Kurland, for allowing us to come to the 'Bird, grab people out of the bar, and off the stage, question 'em, shoot 'em, and hang 'em on your wall.
Mervin Louque, for letting us conduct a large, long meeting at Douglas Corner.
Kevin Bradley and Jim Sherraden at Hatch Show Print and Mike Walker for doing spectacular work in literally no time.
Michael Gomez for all the assisting, stunt photography, advice and psychological counseling, and especially that really long extension cord!
And especially to all the songwriters who came to meet us - sometimes under rather strange circumstances - and let us in on their life stories.